Wrapagami

The Art of Fabric Gift Wraps

Wrapagami

Jennifer Playford

founder of Furochic™

ST. MARTIN'S GRIFFIN
NEW YORK

Wrapagami

For information, address St. Martin's Press, 175 Fifth Avenue, New York, NY 10010.

www.stmartins.com

A Quirk Packaging Book

Design by woolypear

Editing by Erin Slonaker

Illustrations by Nancy Leonard

Library of Congress Cataloging-in-Publication Data Available Upon Request

ISBN-13: 978-0-312-56667-8

ISBN-10: 0-312-56667-0

First Edition: August 2009

10 9 8 7 6 5 4 3 2 1

Dedication

To Grandma and Grand Jim, for the love you shower on me, your creative influence, and your inspiration.

Acknowledgments

All the squares (excluding Furochic™) were expertly cut and sewn by Korinne, the Queen of Patchwork. Thank you also for the handy patchwork tips.

For her ongoing, insightful, creative advice, I would like to thank Chrystal.

A big thank you to Scott, Ava, and Oliver, who gave me treasured time to work on this book and for their constant inspiration. xoxoxo

To my mom for my creative side and to my dad for my business side, both of which I use every day in my entrepreneurial endeavors.

Thank you to Sharyn Rosart, everyone at Quirk Packaging, and BJ and St. Martin's Press for making *Wrapagami* happen and for being so lovely to work with.

Contents

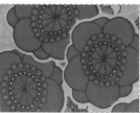

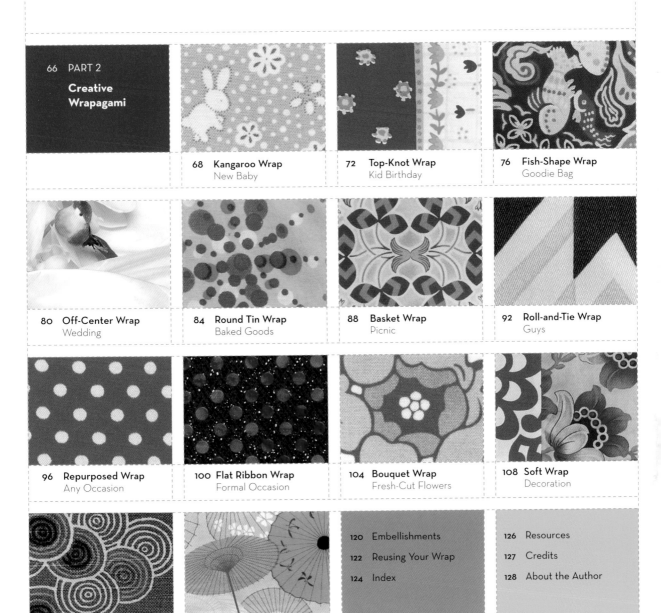

Introduction

I love fabric. Walking into a store where the shelves are filled with beautiful fabrics makes my heart race with anticipation, and the gorgeous colors, textures, and patterns are always invigorating and inspiring. I have always enjoyed making things using my vast collection of fabric, ribbon, yarn, trinkets, gems, and odds and ends—and, especially, using these embellishments to decorate gifts. For years, pages from fashion magazines were my gift wrap of choice, as I felt that wrapping paper was wasteful. Eventually, my love for textiles and concerns about the environment prompted me to try wrapping gifts with fabric remnants from my collection.

An interest in Japanese art and design, especially textiles, led me to *furoshiki*, a cloth wrap used in Japan since the seventeenth century to wrap and carry items. From there it was a small step to creating Furochic™ wraps, a modern interpretation of the Japanese tradition. (For more information about furoshiki and Furochic™, see pages 9–11.)

Wrapagami brings all of these interests together in a beautiful, practical, how-to book on wrapping with fabric. Drawing on the Japanese traditions of *tsutsumi*, or wrapping, *Wrapagami* shows how to use any square piece of fabric to make beautiful, environmentally friendly, reusable gift wraps that work for any occasion.

Wrapping with fabric has so many advantages that I am confident you will love it as much as I do. It's easy—and the step-by-step instructions in this book make it virtually foolproof. It requires no cutting or tape—and it's much more forgiving than paper: If you make a mistake, simply unwrap and start again! It's green—wrapping with fabric saves trees and prevents waste. Best of all, each wrap is a gift in itself, so it's like getting two presents at once! The lucky recipient can reuse the wrap in numerous ways, including to wrap a gift for someone else, thereby passing on this wonderful craft. (See pages 122–123 for lots of fantastic wrap reuses.)

Part 1—*Basic Wraps*—shows wrapping techniques for a variety of shapes and sizes; Part 2—*Creative Wraps*—offers special wraps for particular occasions. I had so much fun creating each of these wraps, and I hope these projects inspire you to try your own versions—and, most importantly, to have fun doing it!

—Jennifer Playford

Furoshiki to Furochic™

NARA PERIOD (EIGHTH CENTURY)

Starting in the eighth century, a square piece of fabric called *hokei-fuhaku* was used to wrap special items of value, including clothing for Buddhist priests and elaborate minstrel costumes. The wrapping was called *tsutsumi*, and its main purpose was to protect and carry garments.

EDO PERIOD (1603–1868)

As bathhouses increased in popularity, the square wrap became known as *furoshiki*: *furo* meaning "bath" and *shiki* meaning "to spread." Furoshiki were used to carry toiletries and clothing to the bathhouses and were also placed on the floor to act as bathmats.

During this period, wealthy families commissioned bridal furoshiki of different sizes, decorated with their family crests and symbols of good luck.

1800s

When cotton was introduced from overseas, furoshiki began to be produced on a larger scale. At the same time, people of Japan were traveling more for pleasure, often selling goods along the way. Furoshiki were used for not only transporting the travelers' belongings but also their goods for sale.

1900s

At the turn of the twentieth century, the advances in textile production—mainly automated looms from overseas—made furoshiki even more accessible to the public. Furoshiki became mass-produced, and the tradition of using cloth to wrap gifts was established. Gifts wrapped with furoshiki would often be presented in person; the person giving the gift would unwrap and reveal the gift, and then keep the cloth to take home.

The bridal furoshiki also became commonplace, and the bride used the large cloths for wrapping her belongings and the small cloths for wrapping gifts.

POST-WORLD WAR II

After World War II, the Japanese became more highly influenced by American culture, resulting in the decline of furoshiki. The invention of the paper bag, followed by the plastic bag and the emergence of supermarkets across Japan in the 1970s, contributed to the disappearance of furoshiki. Plastic boxes and bags replaced furoshiki as a means of storage and for carrying goods. By the 1980s, the custom of using furoshiki to wrap gifts had declined almost to obscurity.

1990s–PRESENT

When Japan's economic boom ended in the early 1990s, people began to reflect upon the disadvantages and waste in a disposable society.

In 2006, Japan's then Minister of the Environment, Ms. Yuriko Koike, launched a campaign to encourage the use of furoshiki, instead of paper and plastic, and bring back the cultural tradition of wrapping and carrying items in fabric. She designed a furoshiki called the "Mottainai Furoshiki," *mottainai*, translating to "waste not, want not."

The result has been a renewed and widespread interest in the tradition of tsutsumi and a flowering of creativity associated with it. Furoshiki are beginning to be seen outside of Japan as people worldwide embrace greener lifestyles and adapt different cultural solutions to their own ways of living.

FUROSHIKI

Furoshiki come in various sizes but are always square. Oversized furoshiki are called *o-buroshiki* and can be large enough to wrap a futon; miniature furoshiki are used in tea ceremonies.

There are three basic ways to wrap with furoshiki: *fukusa-tsutsumi,* when the cloth is simply folded around the gift, is commonly used for small gifts or monetary gifts in envelopes, *otsukai-tsutsumi* refers to wraps that have been knotted once, and *yotsu-musubi* uses two knots or double handles for heavier items.

As with kimono fabric, furoshiki were traditionally designed with motifs that held meaning, reflecting the occasion and significance of the gift. Today, the majority of furoshiki have traditional Japanese imagery, but there are also modern versions in bright and graphic prints.

JAPANESE IMAGERY

MOTIF	MEANING	OCCASION
Chrysanthemum	Longevity, Good Fortune	Wedding
Carp Swimming	Strength, Perseverance	Congratulations
Treasure Trove	Happiness, Prosperity	Birthday
Pine and Bamboo	Longevity, Endurance	Anniversary
Plum Blossom	New Hope	New Baby
Crane	Longevity	Wedding
Cherry Blossom	Treasure the Moment	Spring Birthday
Family Crests	Heritage	Wedding
Tortoise	Longevity	Housewarming
Purple Patterns	Dignity, Nobility	Graduation
Maple Leaves	Abundance	Fall Birthday

FUROCHIC™

Furochic™ is my interpretation of furoshiki and is a fabric gift wrap based on my designs. It naturally evolved from my interest in Japanese textiles, the enthusiastic response my fabric-wrapped gifts received, and the delight I felt when giving a piece of fabric that I loved to someone else to enjoy. (For more information on Furochic™, visit www.furochic.com.)

Getting Started

The projects in *Wrapagami* have been made using Furochic™ and other sourced fabrics (see "Credits," page 127) that were cut into squares and topstitched to finish the edges (see "Making Your Own Wrap," opposite). Whether you buy a finished wrap or make your own, here are some helpful tips:

CHOOSING YOUR FABRIC AND WRAP STYLE

A good wrap should be the right weight of fabric that is opaque enough to conceal the gift, yet thin enough to tie nice knots. If the fabric is too thick, the knots will be bulky and difficult to tie; if the fabric is too lightweight, the ends of the wrap won't hold their shape and will droop. A thicker fabric can be used for the folded wraps (fukusa-tsutsumi), as there are no knots involved. The shape of the gift will determine which style of wrap to use.

FIGURING OUT YOUR WRAP SIZE

You can refer to the size tips below, or measure your gift's length, which should be approximately one-third the size of the diagonal measurement of the wrap from corner to corner. If the wrap is too large, it may look baggy, and the ends of the knots will be far too large; if it is too small, the gift will poke out and be revealed. Furoshiki come in sizes ranging from 18" to 52" square (45.5 to 132 cm square) without seams. The most common size is 28" square (71 cm square).

Small Wrap: 18" to 24" (45.5 to 61 cm)
A jewelry box, a paperback book, a mobile phone, a box of chocolates, stationery, a gift envelope

Medium Wrap: 28" to 30" (71 to 76 cm)
A bottle of wine, a hardcover book, clothing, a bouquet of flowers, a package of food

Large Wrap: 36" to 42" (91.5 to 106.5 cm)
2 bottles of wine, 2 books, a ball

Extra-Large Wrap: 48" to 52" (122 to 132 cm)
A picnic basket, a blanket, a picture frame

REUSING YOUR WRAP

You will be amazed at how versatile a square piece of fabric can be and how many ways there are to reuse your wrap. For resourceful ideas, see pages 122–123.

CARING FOR YOUR WRAP

You may have to iron your wrap to flatten the wrinkles where the fabric was knotted (if reusing a wrap). For cotton, iron on top of the fabric; for synthetics and silk, place a cloth on top of the fabric and then iron.

Making Your Own Wrap

1. Decide your wrap size and add ½" (1.3 cm) on all four sides for finishing. Fabric is typically sold as 42" or 54" (106.5 or 137 cm) wide.

2. Cut fabric into a perfect square. For a quick wrap, use pinking shears to cut out the square. This will prevent the edges from fraying and works especially well for a casual country look.

3. Fold edges over ¼" (0.6 cm) onto the wrong side and iron. Fold over ¼" (0.6 cm) again and iron.

4. For the corners, unfold the edges and trim off the corner diagonally across from the second fold line.

5. Fold the corner edge over by ¼" (0.6 cm) and iron. Refold the straight edges and iron again to finish the corner.

6. Topstitch using a thread that blends into the colors in the wrap.

Fundamentals

One of the pleasures of wrapping with fabric is the gathers that organically form. Try to pleat and gather evenly, occasionally adjusting the fabric until the folds lie neatly. Most wraps start with the wrap lying flat on a diagonal and the gift being placed in the center.

There are two main ways to tie secure and attractive knots when wrapping with fabric: the square knot and the single knot. It is important to tie firm knots, especially for the gift bag and carry bag wraps, so they don't come undone. The knots should be tied approximately 2 to 3 inches (5 to 7.5 cm) from the corners to look more appealing.

SQUARE KNOT

1. Cross "a" over "b."

2. Wrap "a" around "b." Pull ends to lengthen slightly.

3. Cross "a" and "b" again, pulling "a" through hole for the second half of the knot.

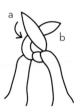

4. Pull "a" and "b" to the left and right to tighten the knot.

SINGLE KNOT

1. Pull one corner of the wrap out while holding the wrap firmly with the other hand.

2. Cross the corner over, making a loop.

3. Bring the corner through the loop.

4. Pull upward to tighten the knot.

TWISTING

Many of the projects require twisting the fabric to make handles. Care should be taken to twist with even gathers and tightness for the most attractive and durable handles.

1. Hold the cloth near the knot with one hand and rotate the cloth above the knot around the index finger. Twist finger over the fabric while using the thumb as a support and to keep the tension even.

2. Finish twisting with enough fabric left over to tie a single knot.

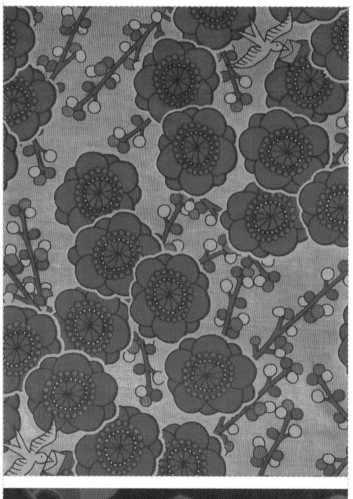

Basic Wrapagami

With a few easy-to-follow steps, you will be able to learn the fundamental wraps and get a feel for the versatility and enjoyment of Basic Wrapagami. This section demonstrates wraps that work well for boxes, books, bottles, tubes, and carry bags. These wraps derive from the original Japanese styles.

Basic Box Wrap

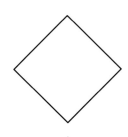

Otsukai Tsutsumi

An excellent way to start, the Basic Box Wrap is quick and easy. You will feel like a pro in no time! It involves just one knot and wraps up neatly and prettily. The flap can be part of the design or be tucked under the knot. When all else fails, this versatile wrap will always come to the rescue. It is great for the holiday season, when you have a large number of gifts to wrap and a little amount of time to wrap them.

What you need

1 square wrap. Size depends on size of box. A 28"x 28" (71 x 71 cm) wrap works for a box that is approximately 12"x 9"x 3" (30.5 x 23 x 7.5 cm).

What to wrap

Perfect for rectangular-shaped boxes or books.

Fabric notes

Lightweight, but opaque, cotton or linen works well. This wrap looks particularly nice with a busy or colorful print, as the wrap is very simple.

Tips + variations

Add a matching gift tag to your wrap that acts as a card and enhances the presentation. Like the pictured wrap, you can make your own tag from scratch or decorate a plain tag from a craft store. Try adding a ribbon that matches the colors in the wrap. Most card shops carry blank tags.

How to do it

1. Lay wrap flat on a diagonal and place box in the center.

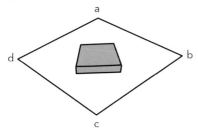

2. Bring corner "a" over the box and tuck it underneath.

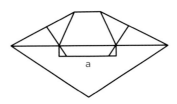

3. Bring corner "c" over the gift, but don't tuck it under. If the corner seems too long, fold more fabric under the gift in step 2.

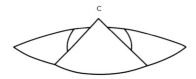

4. Bring "d" and "b" up and arrange gathers evenly.

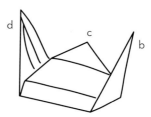

5. Cross "b" and "d" and tie into a firm square knot in the center of the box.

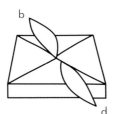

6. Adjust fabric as needed.

4-Tie Box Wrap

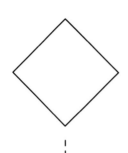

Yotsu Musubi

The 4-Tie Box Wrap is simple yet elegant. It is perhaps the easiest wrap, because no folding is required. This wrap can hold almost any square box securely, and it works equally well for small or large and light or heavy packages. You can even carry the box from the top, holding it under the knots as a handle. The knots on top of the box give the illusion of a fancy bow.

What you need

1 square wrap. The size should be large enough to have 5" (12.5 cm) left after tying the knots. A 28"x 28" (71 x 71 cm) wrap works well for a 6"x 6"x 4" (15 x 15 x 10 cm) box.

What to wrap

Perfect for square boxes.

Fabric notes

Almost any fabric will work, but if your box is heavy, it is best to avoid stretch fabric. Stay away from fabrics that are too thick, or the double knots will be bulky.

Tips + variations

This wrap works well with a scarf that has a 5" (12.5 cm) border. The wrap above has a solid color border, which looks like a separate element sitting on top of the box—a big, complementary bow.

Tuck a note, card, or photo beneath the first (lower) bow for a surprise when the recipient opens the gift.

How to do it

1. Lay wrap flat on a diagonal and place box in the center.

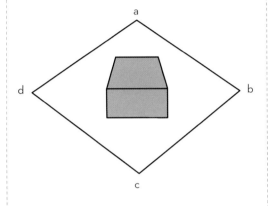

2. Pull up "b" and "d" and center above the box while arranging gathers evenly. Tie a square knot.

3. Adjust corners of first knot. Turn box and pull "a" and "c" up, arranging gathers evenly. Tie a square knot above the first knot.

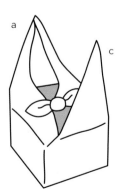

4. Adjust bow corners so that there is one flap in each of the four directions.

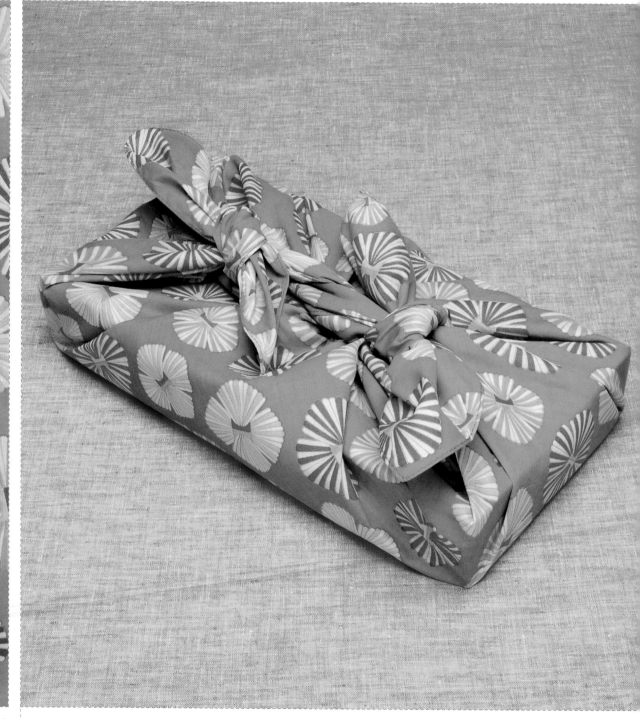

Double-Knot Box Wrap

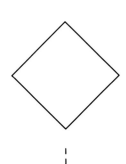

Futatsu Tsutsumi

The Double-Knot Box Wrap is a simple way to make a fancy-looking package. The two knots add embellishment and replace the need for extra ribbons and bows. They also do a good job of holding the wrap together—a useful deterrent for peekers!

Check out the Slender Box Wrap on page 30 for another variation on this elegant wrap.

What you need

1 square wrap. The box shouldn't be placed closely to the corners of the wrap. A 28"x 28" (71 x 71 cm) wrap works well for an 18"x 5"x 4" (45.5 x 12.5 x 10 cm) box.

What to wrap

Long, rectangular shapes are best.

Fabric notes

Silk can be a beautiful choice for this wrap. For a less costly option with a similar feel, try Japanese chirimen crêpe in cotton or rayon.

Tips + variations

The double knots can hold all kinds of fun enhancements, from chopsticks to colored pencils. The chopsticks in the wrap above reflect the long, narrow shape of the package. Each pair slips under a knot, which holds it in place.

Other long objects that work well tucked under the double knots are silk flowers, fans, pens, or pinwheels.

How to do it

1. Lay wrap flat on a diagonal and place box in the center.

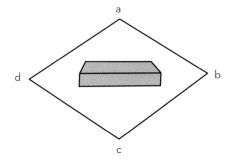

2. Bring "a" and "c" into the center and cross over, bringing "a" toward "d" and "c" toward "b."

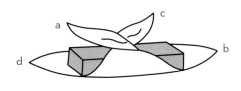

3. Tie "a" and "d" together with a square knot. Tie "c" and "b" together with a square knot.

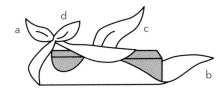

4. Position the knots away from the ends of the box.

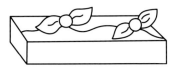

Slender Box Wrap

Kousa Tsutsumi

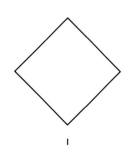

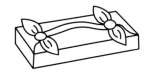

The Slender Box Wrap is the sister wrap to the Double-Knot Box Wrap (page 26). It also has two small knots but is wrapped using a different technique. What makes this wrap special is that after you tie both knots, you end up with a fantastically useful handle that can be used to carry your package. You can keep the wrap flat or transform it into a cute handbag.

What you need

1 square wrap. A 28"x 28" (71 x 71 cm) wrap is ideal for a wallet that is 10"x 4½" x ½" (25.5 x 11.5 x 1.5 cm)

What to wrap

Long, slender objects, such as a man's necktie, a pair of gloves, or a long wallet. This wrap is also good for flat objects.

Fabric notes

A non-stretch fabric, like cotton, works well for this wrap. The fabric must be strong enough to hold the gift by the handle; otherwise, you will end up with a very long bag.

Tips + variations

It is most fun to use this wrap as a carry bag, so why not decorate the handles? For the pictured wrap, I used a ribbon that contrasts with the fabric and tied it with a bow around one of the knots.

Twist the ribbon over the handle, creating a pretty stripe effect. When you reach the second knot, simply wrap the ribbon around the knot and tie a knot on the inside of the handle. Cut any remaining ribbon.

How to do it

1. Lay wrap flat as a square and place box in the center.

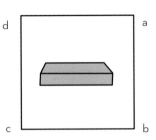

2. Cross "a" and "b" and tie into a square knot in the center of the gift, away from the edges of the object.

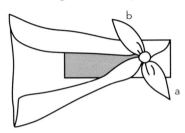

3. Bring "c" under the first knot and pull through. Pull as much fabric through as you can.

4. Bring "c" over to "d" and tie another square knot the same distance from the edge of the object as the first knot.

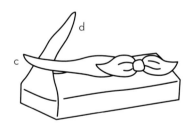

5. Adjust as necessary. Leave flat or pull handle up, changing the shape into a carry bag.

Single Book Wrap

Sao Tsutsumi

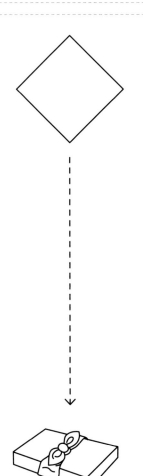

Calling all book lovers: The Single Book Wrap is for you! It is a smart way to protect and carry your favorite book or to give it to another reader. The wrap ties securely about your package with a tidy bow that doubles as a carrying handle. It's also incredibly versatile and can be dressed up or down, depending on the fabric you choose. A practical benefit of this wrap is an extra layer of padding achieved by positioning the book at one corner of the fabric and double wrapping it.

What you need

1 square wrap. A 28"x 28" (71 x 71 cm) wrap works well for a 5"x 8"x 1" (12.5 x 20 x 2.5 cm) book. If the book is wider than 5" (12.5 cm), the fabric won't be long enough to tie a knot.

Ideally you want the fabric to wrap 2 to 4 times around the object.

What to wrap

This wrap is perfect for books, rectangular packages, and boxes containing fragile items that need extra padding.

Fabric notes

Lightweight cotton is a good choice. Avoid fabric that is too thick—the object is wrapped multiple times, and it will be difficult to tie the bow at the end with a thick fabric.

Tips + variations

Tuck a surprise gift or card under the knot. A gift card to a local coffee shop would be a nice addition to a wrapped book, implying a relaxing afternoon reading and sipping tea.

A nice bookmark can slide under the knot, or clip a book light onto the fabric, like the wrap above.

How to do it

1. Lay wrap flat on a diagonal and place book with wide edge toward corner "c." Tuck corner "c" under the book and roll book toward "a."

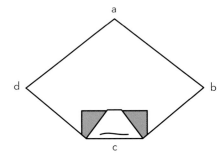

2. Fold corner "a" under the wrap so that it does not go beyond the other side of the book. Bring "d" and "b" up.

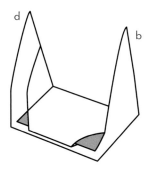

3. Cross "b" and "d" in the center of the book and bring them around each other.

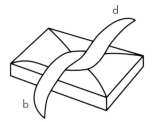

4. Tie "b" and "d" into a tight square knot in the center of the book.

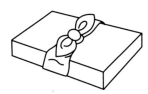

Double Book Wrap

Hon Tsutsumi

Can't get enough of books? Then this Double Book Wrap is for you. Carry two books (or any pair of similarly sized items) in one hand, courtesy of the ingenious hinged handle that distinguishes this wrap. Its clever construction is sure to elicit admiring comments, yet it is quite simple to do. Wrapping two objects in one piece of fabric is convenient and earth-friendly—it's easy to carry and no plastic bags are required.

What you need

1 square wrap. To determine the right size, place the two books side by side in the center of the wrap (set diagonally), then turn the books over once each to the left and right (see step 1). There should be just enough fabric remaining to fold the corners over the books, tucking them underneath the books. A 40"x 40" (1x1 m) wrap works well with books that are approximately 8"x 10"x 1" (20 x 25.5 x 2.5 cm).

What to wrap

This wrap is made for books but can also work for notepads, CDs, DVDs, or any gift that is relatively flat and comes in multiples.

Fabric notes

Choose a sturdy, non-stretch fabric that can hold the weight of two books.

Tips + variations

Suggest to the recipient of your gift that they carry their books to the park and use the wrap to sit on while they read under a tree.

Try an unconventional card by slipping your message inside a luggage tag, as depicted above, which can be reused.

The Double Book Wrap is a great way to give a magazine subscription. Wrap up two magazines and tuck the subscription notice into the gift card.

How to do it

1. Lay wrap flat on a diagonal and place books side by side in the center. Turn books over, once each to the left and right. Fold "d" and "b" over the books, tucking any extra fabric underneath the books.

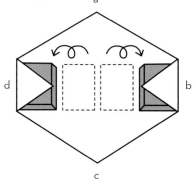

2. Fold books toward center of wrap until they meet.

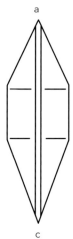

3. Turn the wrap 90 degrees. Cross "a" and "c." While still holding "a" and "c," fold the top book over the bottom book so that the crossed material from "a" and "c" are on the inside, between the books.

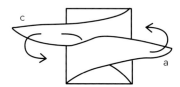

4. Flip the set of books up and stand them on their ends. Take "a" and "c" and twist each one, making a handle. Tie a firm square knot over the center of the package.

Single Bottle Wrap

Bin Tsutsumi

Presenting a special bottle often poses a gift-wrapping dilemma. A plastic bag does not reflect the quality of your gift, while paper bottle bags are wasteful. The Single Bottle Wrap creates the perfect solution. This wrap is elegant and has a convenient handle so you don't have to clutch the bottle under your arm. Upon opening the wrap, the hostess can reuse it immediately as a small tablecloth!

What you need

1 square wrap, 28"x 28" (71 x 71 cm).

What to wrap

Any bottle—a drinkable gift such as wine, champagne, sake, lemonade, or even a fancy sparkling water. Or try kitchen favorites like olive oil or vinegar.

Fabric notes

Almost any fabric works for this wrap; if the bottle is heavy, choose a heavyweight fabric for security.

Tips + variations

For a quick, simple, and no-knot version of the Single Bottle Wrap, bring all four corners of the wrap to the top of the bottle, arranging the gathers neatly and tucking in excess fabric. Like the pictured wrap, tie a matching ribbon into a bow around the neck of the bottle. To help secure the wrap onto the bottle, fasten an elastic band around the neck before tying the ribbon. A 28"x 28" (71 x 71 cm) wrap will fit over a standard bottle, leaving enough fabric for the corners to stand up, creating four pretty petals.

How to do it

1. Lay wrap flat on a diagonal and stand bottle in the center.

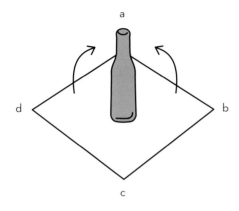

2. Bring "b" and "d" over the top of the bottle and cross over into a half-square knot. Twist the corners tightly.

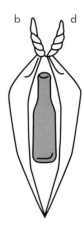

3. Tie a small, firm square knot.

4. Turn the bottle and cross "a" and "c" around the back of the bottle to the front.

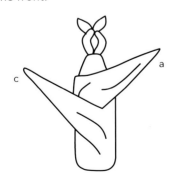

5. Tie a square knot in the center front of the bottle.

Double Bottle Wrap

Bin Tsutsumi II

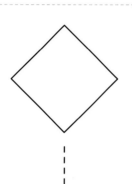

You will be the most popular person at the party when you show up with two bottles of wine wrapped in the gorgeous Double Bottle Wrap. The extra padding of the wrap protects the bottles, preventing them from knocking into each other. The handle is especially strong and secure in this wrap, enabling you to carry the weight of two bottles with confidence.

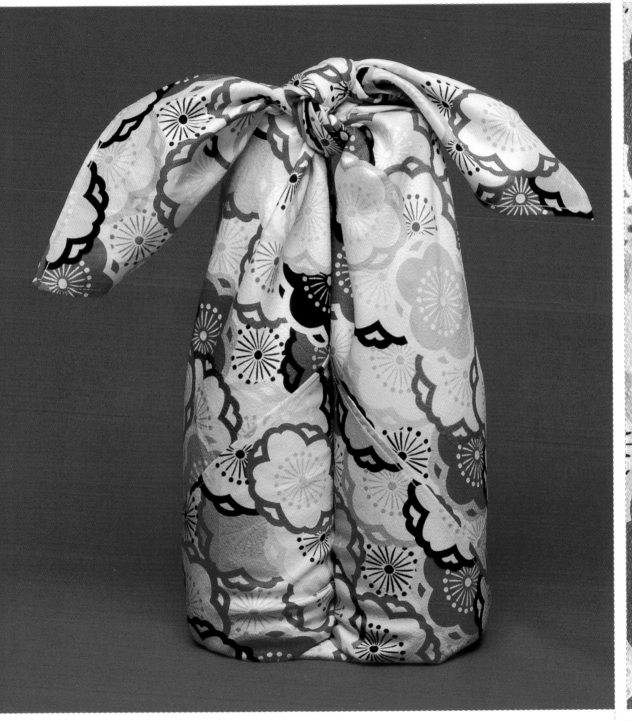

What you need

1 square wrap, 36" x 36"
(91.5 x 91.5 cm).

What to wrap

Perfect for matched bottles,
from oil and vinegar to shampoo
and conditioner!

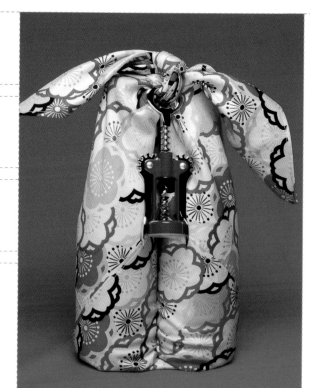

Fabric notes

A thick, strong cotton is best
to hold the weight of the two
bottles. Bamboo fabric, which is
both strong and eco-conscious,
is becoming increasingly popular
and would also work well.

Tips + variations

How many times has the corkscrew gone
missing at a party? Avoid frustration and
impress your host by attaching a corkscrew to the wrap before you tie the final
knot. Buy the kind that has a bottle opener
at the top; the hole will be large enough to
slide onto the tie. After tying the knot, the
corkscrew should hang in the middle of
the bottles like the one above.

How to do it

1. Lay wrap flat on a diagonal and stand bottles in the middle of the cloth. Lay bottles down about 4" (10 cm) apart, with the necks of the bottles facing out.

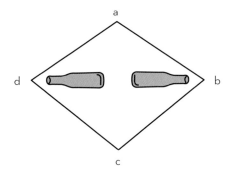

2. Bring corner "c" over the bottles and then roll the bottles up toward "a."

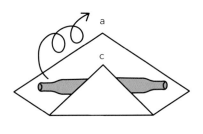

3. Once the bottles are tightly rolled, bring "b" and "d" upward until bottles are standing.

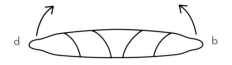

4. Tie "b" and "d" together into a square knot.

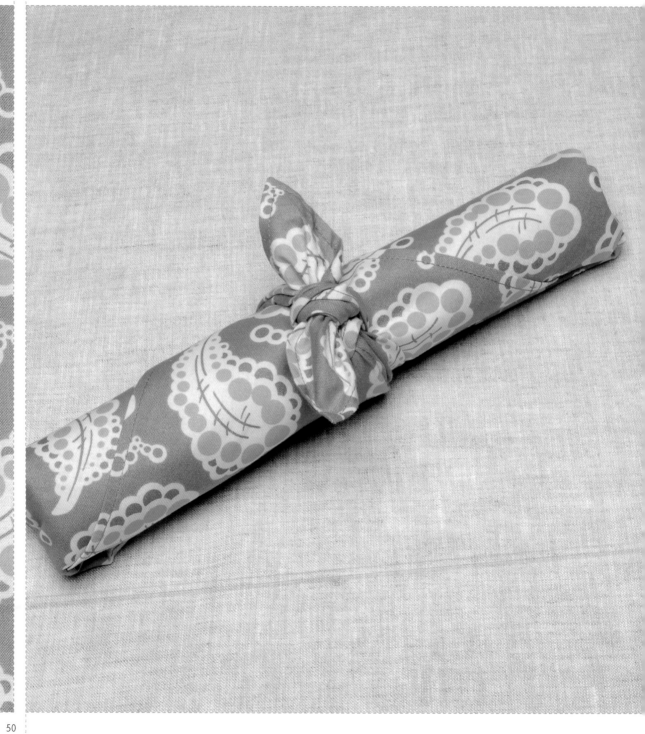

Candlestick Wrap

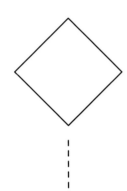

Entou Tsutsumi

The functional and attractive Candlestick Wrap makes wrapping cylindrical objects easy. A poster tube is unnecessary with this wrap, which has ample padding, as the object is rolled multiple times before it is tied. A tidy little bow adds a nice touch while holding the wrap in place.

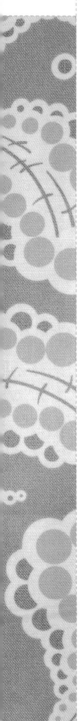

What you need

1 square wrap. A 28"x 28" (71 x 71 cm) wrap works well for a standard-size magazine. A poster that is 30" (76 cm) long will need a 48"x48" (1.2 x 1.2 m) wrap.

What to wrap

Cylindrical objects or items that roll: posters, maps, children's art, yoga mats, magazines, and prints. As the name implies, this wrap is great for candles and candlesticks.

This wrap can also wrap clothing after it is rolled into a tube shape, and it is handy for storing documents.

Fabric notes

Any fabric will work for this wrap. Lightweight fabric is especially useful because the object is rolled many times.

Tips + variations

If you don't have enough fabric to tie a square knot in steps 3 and 4, try the Half-Candlestick Wrap. Follow steps 1 and 2 and then tie corners "b" and "d" into a square knot. The pair of candlesticks pictured above was wrapped this way and decorated with two tapered candles held in place under the knot.

How to do it

1. Lay wrap flat on a diagonal and place tube near corner "c." Roll "c" over the tube and continue to roll toward corner "a."

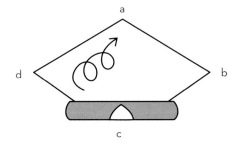

2. Roll entire wrap until it is completely around the tube.

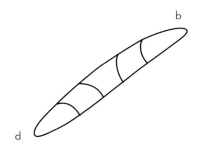

3. Fold "b" to the left and "d" to the right and cross over in the center of the tube.

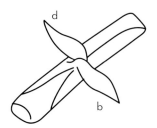

4. Bring "b"and "d" around the front and tie into a square knot.

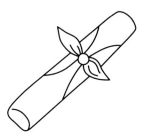

Standard Carry Wrap

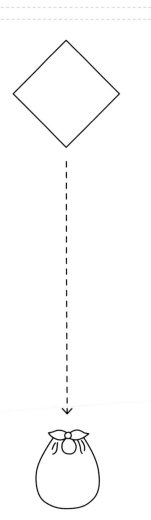

Tesage Bukuro

The Standard Carry Wrap is the earth-friendly alternative to the paper gift bag stuffed with tissue. It is a terrific way to present a medley of small gifts, and it is very easy to make. Being one of the most versatile wraps, it can be relied on for most occasions, especially daily shopping excursions.

What you need

1 square wrap. A 28"x 28" (71 x 71 cm) wrap works well for a small bag, but feel free to go larger with this handy wrap.

What to wrap

Multiple small objects fit inside this gift bag nicely. Try a collection of toiletries, small food items, or kitchen gadgets—even a set of tools! It is fine if a larger item is poking out the top; it will intrigue the recipient.

Tips + variations

If you have a lightweight fabric, try lining it with a plain cotton broadcloth to thicken it. You can layer the two wraps, one on top of the other, before tying. The double layer will add another dimension and make the wrap reversible.

Try the Handle Wrap (see instructions opposite) for a carry bag that can double as a stylish purse. Use two round handles that are 5" (12.5 cm) in diameter. Purse handles can be found at craft shops, or large bangles will suffice.

Fabric notes

Choose a thick cotton or linen strong enough to hold the contents. For an elegant bag, use silk or taffeta.

How to do it

STANDARD CARRY WRAP

1. Lay wrap flat as a square. Bring the two left corners together and tie a square knot. Bring the two right corners together and tie a square knot.

2. Adjust the gathers and knots and fluff the bag into a nice shape. Tuck the excess left and right sides of the wrap inside the bag.

HANDLE WRAP

1. Bring the left corner of the wrap through the handle, from the front to the back. Pull the corner to the left and then to the front of the bag. Repeat with the right corner, bringing it through and to the right.

2. Tie the two corners into a firm square knot in front of the bag. Repeat step 1 with the two remaining corners and the other handle. Adjust gathers and knots and fluff the bag into a nice shape, tucking some of the excess fabric inside. The bag is now ready to fill with gifts.

Watermelon Wrap

Suika Tsutsumi

Disguise a large, round object in this appropriately named Watermelon Wrap. The long handle makes it easy to carry or to hang on a hook. Choose a bright and cheery fabric or a classic red-and-white gingham, and bring it to a picnic or barbecue. The wrap can then be reused as a tablecloth or picnic blanket.

What you need

1 square wrap. A 38"x 38" (1 x 1 m) wrap works well for a sphere that is 25" (63.5 cm) in diameter. If wrapping a globe, you will need a much larger wrap, closer to 52"x 52" (1.3 x 1.3 m).

What to wrap

Large, round objects—balls, melons, lanterns, and globes.

Tips + variations

Use a 28"x 28" (71 x 71 cm) wrap to create the Mini-Watermelon Wrap, pictured above, which is great for carrying soccer balls to practice by its small carry handle.

Make a Standard Carry Wrap from page 54, place the ball in the bag, and bring one handle through the other handle, which holds the ball securely and leaves a small handle for carrying.

Fabric notes

Use a thick, sturdy, non-stretch fabric if you intend to use your wrap for melons or other heavy, large objects; otherwise, cotton or linen will work.

How to do it

1. Lay wrap flat and place the ball in the center.

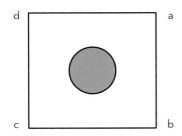

2. Tie "a" and "d" into a square knot over the ball.

3. Bring "b" and "c" through the knot, pulling tightly to cover the ball.

4. Twist "b" and "c" into handles.

5. Tie "b" and "c" into a square knot.

Over-the-Shoulder Wrap

Katakake Fukuro

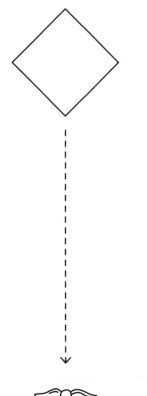

The Over-the-Shoulder Wrap is simple yet functional. Three knots (two hidden) hold it in place and leave room for the bag to slide over a shoulder. Inside, there is ample room for items of varying sizes. It's a great way to wrap a gift for the crafty person on your list—fill it with yarns and other knitting and crochet supplies. This wrap can be easily reused because it holds its shape even after the gift is "unwrapped."

What you need

1 square wrap. The wrap has to be at least 36"x 36" (91.5 x 91.5 cm) to sit over the shoulder; otherwise, it will be more of a handbag.

What to wrap

This wrap is so versatile—a super choice for either an assortment of small gifts or one large gift. It's ideal for multiples because the bag is deep and holds the contents securely inside.

Fabric notes

A strong, durable fabric such as a thick cotton or denim is best. If the fabric is too flimsy, it won't hold its shape and may tear when carrying heavier items. Try a thick embroidered Chinese silk for a more formal look.

Tips + variations

For an extra-secure version of this wrap, the Handbag Wrap, above, closes completely. Make sure to place your gift inside before tying the final knot!

How to do it

OVER-THE-SHOULDER WRAP

1. Lay wrap flat on a diagonal and fold "c" up toward "a" to form a triangle.

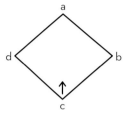

2. Gather corner "d" and measure approximately ½ the length of the side of the triangle. Tie into a single knot. Repeat the same for "b."

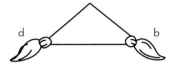

3. Flip the wrap inside out so that the two knots are sitting inside of the bag. Hold "a" and "c" up.

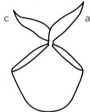

4. Tie "a" and "c" into a square knot. Adjust fabric and gathers and place your gift inside the bag.

HANDBAG WRAP

Follow steps 1 to 3.

4. Instead of tying a square knot, tie a half-square knot and pull on the ends until the opening of the purse closes over with fabric.

5. Twist the two ends and tie in a square knot to complete the handle.

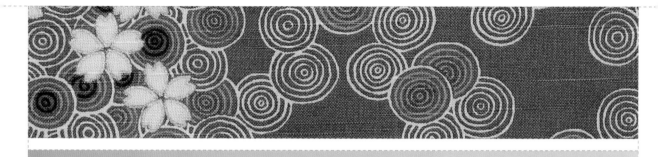

PART 2

Now that you've become comfortable with Basic Wrapagami, *it's* time to have some *fun!* Using these Creative Wrapagami *ideas* as your guide, let your imagination run wild, whether creating a gift wrap or practical wrap. There are endless decorating possibilities, beginning with toys, trinkets, jewelry, and ribbon, to take any wrap to the next level. Who knows? Maybe you'll design a wrapagami of your own innovation!

Creative Wrapagami

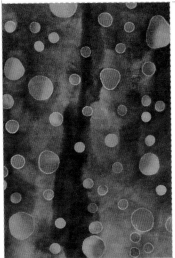

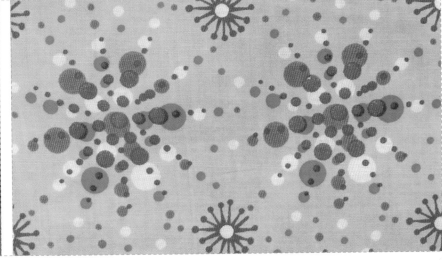

Kangaroo Wrap

New Baby

With its cozy front pouch for tucking in a toy and card, the Kangaroo Wrap is perfect for a baby shower gift. A snuggly, little plush bunny or lamb will make your gift almost as cute as the new arrival! A coordinating ribbon adds a nice accent by decorating the parcel and keeping the contents of the pouch secure. The pouch is roomy and versatile; try tucking in a board book, baby rattle, hat and socks, or a baby toiletry pack.

What you need

1 square wrap. A 30"x30" (76 x 76 cm) wrap is a good size for a box approximately 9"x 9"x 3" (23 x 23 x 7.5 cm).

What to wrap

This wrap is most successful for a square gift that is not too thick. It is ideal for wrapping baby clothes, either in a box or folded into a neat pile. It can also work well for blankets or quilts that are folded into a square. Choose an item that enhances the main gift to tuck into the pouch, such as a stuffed toy, rattle, or small book.

Tips + variations

Embrace the reusable aspect of this wrap by using a receiving blanket. The parents-to-be will thank you! If your blanket is rectangular, simply fold over one end to form a square before you begin wrapping. Like the wrapagami above, enhance the blanket with cute plush toys tucked into the pouch.

Fabric notes

Choose a soft fabric, like cotton, flannel, or fine corduroy, in a solid color or with a cute print. Prints with animals or multi-colored polka dots are great and work for boys and girls.

How to do it

1. Lay wrap flat on a diagonal and place box in the center.

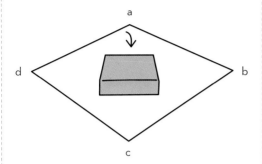

2. Fold "a" over the top of the box so that the corner folds over the side of the box.

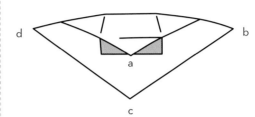

3. Bring "d" and "b" up and tie into a square knot over the center of the box.

4. Wrap corner "c" over the top of the box, over the square knot.

5. Tuck "c" under the knot, pushing the fabric down until a pocket is formed.

Top-Knot Wrap

Kid Birthday

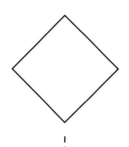

The key to the successful Top-Knot Wrap is that it's easy for kids to untie. They will be delighted at how quickly the knot comes undone, revealing the surprise inside. Kids' birthday presents tend to come in large boxes, and this wrap was designed to be versatile, working with a variety of sizes.

What you need

1 square wrap. A 36"x 36" (91.5 x 91.5 cm) wrap is a good size for a box approximately 9"x 12"x 5" (23 x 30.5 x 12.5 cm). When all four corners are gathered and secured above the center of the box, there should be approximately 10" (25.5 cm) of fabric remaining to twist.

What to wrap

Any medium- to large-sized box. The box can be square or rectangular.

Fabric notes

A lightweight fabric works best for gathering the four corners into one knot. If the birthday party has a theme, try to find a print with a motif that matches. There are lots of fun patterns that appeal to kids and that can find new life afterward as tea-party tablecloths or superhero capes.

Tips + variations

If your fabric is too bulky to secure a single top knot, twist the corners into four mini top knots. Tie the opposite corners into a square knot, twist each corner individually, and weave the ends through the hole in the center. The four knots resemble a fancy bow, and your accessory—as pictured here, a lollipop—slips through the knots or is tied on.

How to do it

1. Lay wrap flat on a diagonal and place box in the center.

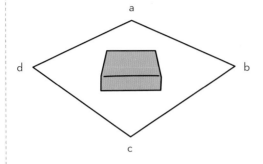

2. Bring all four corners up and gather together over the center of the box.

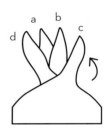

3. Hold the four corners together with your right hand over the center of the box. Using the left hand index finger, twist all four corners together.

4. Wrap fabric around in a circle over the center of the box. Once a complete circle has been formed, weave the end from the bottom to the top through the hole in the center.

5. Pull the end firmly to secure the knot, leaving it poking out or tucking it under the top knot.

Fish-Shape Wrap

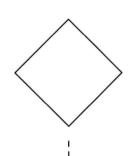

Goodie Bag

The Fish-Shape Wrap is a pouch-style wrap that makes a terrific goodie bag. Make it extra fun by carrying through the party theme—in this case, an undersea motif. A button eye and a toy goldfish complete this fish story, but you can also choose a simple approach, like a color scheme.

What you need

1 square wrap. A 28"x 28" (71 x 71 cm) wrap will hold several small items. Adjust the size of your wrap depending on the size of the goodies inside. Ideally, the tails of the fish should be between 6" (15 cm) and 8" (20 cm) long.

What to wrap

A group of small items that are not fragile or too rigid in shape. The items should be able to move around when you are adjusting the shape of the fish. Anything too large and square will poke out. Try small toys, candy, individual stickers, or marbles.

Fabric notes

The fabric should be stiff enough to hold the shape of the fish tail. Try a thick cotton, linen, or denim. A color and pattern with a fishy or nautical theme is great, but feel free to go with any fun color or pattern that works for your party and goodie selection.

Tips + variations

For a more versatile goodie bag that will work for any party and will hold a large variety of items, use the Standard Carry Wrap from page 54. To conceal the contents of the bag, tie the handles together with a trinket attached, like the rubber goldfish above.

How to do it

1. Lay wrap flat on a diagonal and place small items in a cluster slightly to the right of the center of the wrap.

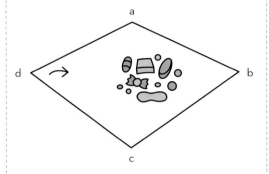

2. Fold wrap in half, bringing "d" over to meet "b."

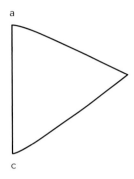

3. Cross "a" and "c" over the top, bringing them to the back. Cross them over the back and bring them around to the front and tie a square knot.

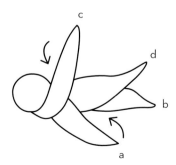

4. Adjust "d" and "b" into the fish tail shape and sew a button as the eye to the front of the wrap. The wrap must lie on its side to maintain the fish shape.

Off-Center Wrap

Wedding

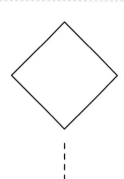

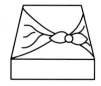

Though many of the wraps draw the eye to the center of the gift or feature symmetrical bows, you can achieve a sophisticated look by tying your knots off to the side. A variation of the Basic Box Wrap (page 18), the Off-Center Wrap is an elegant choice for wrapping gifts for formal occasions. A luxurious fabric, such as this cream dupioni silk, sets the stage for further embellishment—here, a branch of exotic silk orchids and delicate birds give the package an ethereal beauty.

What you need

1 square wrap. A 40"x 40" (1 x 1 m) wrap works well for a box approximately 16"x 12"x 5½" (40.5 x 30.5 x 14 cm).

What to wrap

Any large rectangular or square box. Be sure the box has a wide top, so you'll have enough room to position your knot to one side.

Fabric notes

A lightweight fabric makes it easier to create pretty pleats, gathers, and folds. Dupioni silk drapes well and has a rich, elegant texture. It is available in many colors, so you will have many options to choose from. Solid colors work best if you plan to add embellishments—craft stores usually stock delicate fabric flowers, birds, butterflies, and other nature-inspired decorations.

Tips + variations

Another way to adorn your gift and emphasize the knot's off-center place-ment is by tying a wide contrasting ribbon around the box and attaching an embellishment to the knot—the blue ribbon and butterflies, above, transform this into an elegant package.

For a thoughtful wedding gift, investigate ahead of time what colors and flowers have been chosen for the wedding, and use them in your wrap. The bride and groom will have a keepsake that reminds them of their special day.

How to do it

1. Lay wrap flat on a diagonal and place box vertically in the center with the narrow side facing you.

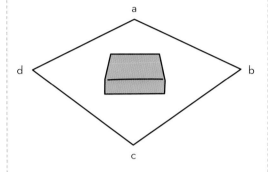

2. Fold "a" over the top of the box until the corner touches the side.

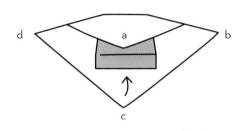

3. Fold the tip of corner "c" over and then fold again over the top of the box. The edge of the fold will dictate where on the box the square knot will sit. If you would like the knot to sit lower, fold over more of corner "c" before folding the edge over the box.

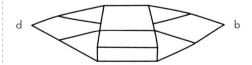

4. Bring "d" and "b" up, making sure to tuck in the fabric neatly at the corners, and tie in a square knot to the right of the box, over the folded edge from step 3. Arrange gathers evenly.

Round Tin Wrap

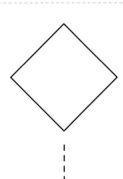

Baked Goods

A gift of home-baked goodies keeps on giving when presented in the Round Tin Wrap. With its loosely tied bow (that doubles as a carrying handle), this wrap highlights the old-fashioned, handmade quality of your gift. Be sure to let the recipient know that the wrap can be reused as a festive tablecloth or to wrap a gift for someone else!

What you need

1 square wrap. A 28"x 28" (71 x 71 cm) wrap works well with a round tin that is 8" (20.5 cm) in diameter and 3½" (9 cm) deep.

What to wrap

This wrap is designed for a round tin (lined with wax paper and filled with home-baked sweets).

Fabric notes

Medium-weight cotton or linen are good choices. For a festive look, try a shiny fabric such as taffeta in rich jewel tones or an embroidered silk with metallic accents.

Tips + variations

For a quick Bundle Wrap without a tin, simply wrap the goodies in wax paper and place in the center of the wrap. Bring all four corners up, like the wrap above, arranging the gathers evenly. Fasten an elastic band around the corners to hold them together. Finally, tie a decorative ribbon into a bow around the elastic band.

How to do it

1. Lay wrap flat on a diagonal and place round tin in the center of the wrap.

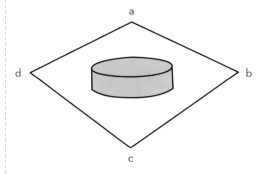

2. Bring all four corners up, arranging the gathers evenly.

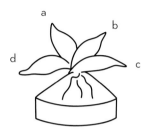

3. Cross "d" and "b" around the back and tie at front using a half-square knot.

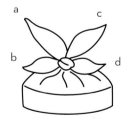

4. Take "a" to the left and "c" to the right and tuck the corners under the half-square knot. Bring "d" and "b" over the center and tie into a square knot. Adjust fabric to form an even bow.

Basket Wrap

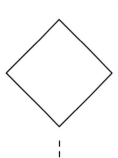

Picnic

One of life's great pleasures is a meal enjoyed outdoors. Place your gourmet-to-go meal in this Basket Wrap, and find a suitable spot for your picnic. Then unwrap, use the cloth as a picnic spread to sit on, and tuck in to your food. Filled with gourmet treats, this wrapped basket also makes a delightful gift.

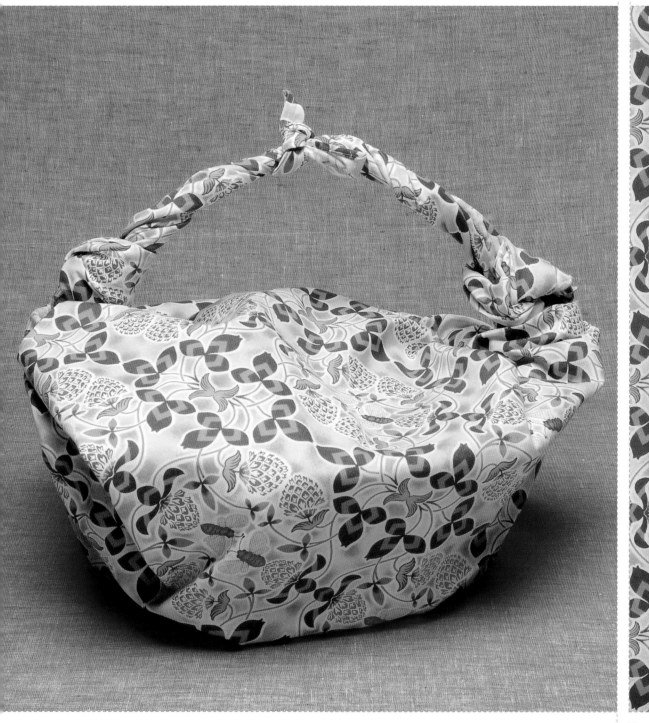

What you need

1 large square wrap and a basket (no handles) or box to hold the food.
A 42"x42" (1 x 1 m) wrap works for a round basket that is 11" (28 cm) in diameter.

What to wrap

A basket full of good things to eat and drink. Note that a bottle of wine or other beverage must lie on its side; otherwise, it will be too tall for the handles. Don't forget to add the essentials: cutlery, a small cutting board, a paring knife, napkins, cups, and a bottle opener.

Tips + variations

For a large basket, try wrapping with a thin picnic blanket, bedspread, or tablecloth. The wrap becomes part of the gift and can be reused over and over again, making this a great choice for a hostess gift.

Red-and-white gingham, as pictured, cut out with pinking shears, is a classic choice for a country-style picnic wrap. You will be able to whip up your wrap in no time and will have a decorative edge that won't unravel.

Fabric notes

A durable fabric like a heavyweight cotton or linen. The fabric must be strong enough to hold the heavy items inside the basket and be thick enough to sit on.

How to do it

1. Lay wrap flat on a diagonal and place basket on top in the center.

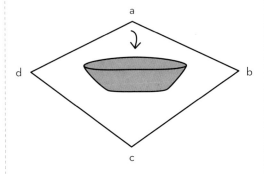

2. Fold corner "a" over the basket to line the inside.

3. Take "d" and "b" and tie the corners into single knots.

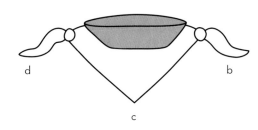

4. Twist "d" and "b" and tie together with a square knot to form a handle. Place picnic items into the basket.

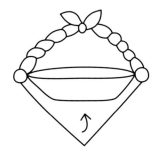

5. Take "c" and fold it over to cover the top of the basket.

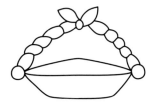

Roll-and-Tie Wrap

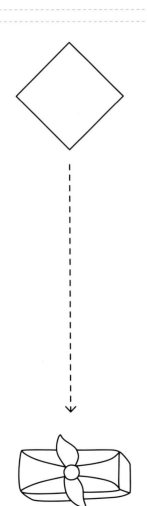

Guys

Give a guy a gift presented in the Roll-and-Tie Wrap, and he gets the added benefit of a wrap of his own. Extremely simple to do, yet thoroughly attractive, this wrap is also both functional and versatile—and it does not require a box. Being able to wrap up any gift so quickly and appealingly is a skill every guy should have.

What you need

1 square wrap. The diagonal measurement of the wrap from corner "a" to "c" must be approximately 3 to 4 times the length of the gift. A 28"x 28" (71 x 71 cm) wrap is appropriate for an item that is approximately 9" (23 cm) long.

What to wrap

This wrap is ideal for narrow items that don't come in a box. The length of the item can vary and will determine the size of the wrap. The wrap should roll over the item 4 to 6 times.

Fabric notes

For a more padded wrap, use a soft, thick fabric such as a heavyweight cotton, tweed, denim, or flannel. If padding isn't an issue, you can use lightweight fabrics like oxford cloth.

Tips + variations

Try wrapping a smaller gift in a bandanna that can be reused. The variation above is wrapped using a traditional bandanna print in red, black, and white. For extra padding, layer two bandannas in contrasting colors, one on top of the other, before rolling the gift.

How to do it

1. Lay wrap flat on a diagonal and place gift toward corner "c."

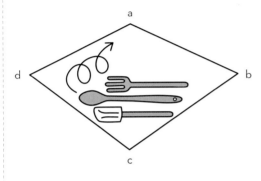

2. Fold "c" over the gift and roll wrap toward "a."

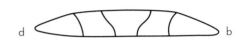

3. Bring "d" and "b" up and tie together into a square knot.

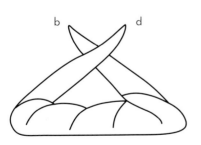

4. Adjust knot and gathers as needed.

Repurposed Wrap

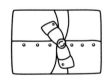

Any Occasion

The Repurposed Wrap is truly eco-friendly, calling for a vintage or second-hand piece of clothing or fabric to be used as the wrap. Scour thrift shops, vintage stores, or your grandparents' closet to find an appropriate piece. Knowing the style of the person you are buying for will make it likelier that the wrap will be reused. Alternatively, choose something kitschy for a laugh. Dress it up by pinning a brooch to the outside or by wrapping an old tie around it.

What you need

1 vintage long-sleeve shirt, with or without buttons.

Safety pins (optional).

What to wrap

The size of your shirt will determine what you can wrap, although most shirts will accommodate a medium-sized, rectangular box. Try a hardcover coffee table book, large photo album, or picture frame. The key is to use a gift that is not too wide; otherwise, the arms won't be long enough to tie around the front.

Fabric notes

A lightweight cotton, silk, or polyester shirt is best and won't be too bulky.

Tips + variations

Vintage scarves are another fantastic option for repurposed wraps. They are often square and come in beautiful designs and various sizes.

The scarf below is lightweight and made of silk, which makes it easy to tie attractive knots.

The 4-Tie Box Wrap variation on page 24 is also great for vintage scarves.

How to do it

1. Lay shirt flat with the front of the shirt facing down. Tuck your gift inside the shirt.

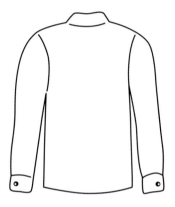

2. Fold the top and bottom of the shirt over the gift. If the shirt doesn't extend far enough, you may use a safety pin to secure the fabric.

3. Cross the sleeves behind the gift and turn gift over.

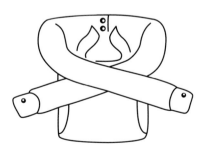

4. Tie the sleeves into a square knot. If your gift is narrow, you may be able to tie the sleeves into a bow.

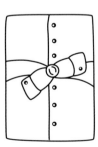

Flat Ribbon Wrap

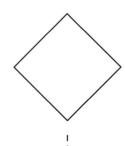

Formal Occasion

The Flat Ribbon Wrap is the only *Creative Wrap* that doesn't require any knots, relying instead upon ribbon for both security and beauty. This technique is the most similar to wrapping with paper and yields a more stream-lined package. The fabric is folded over the gift and held together with a safety pin. Overlays of ribbon add beauty and function. This wrap is an excellent way to use up scraps of luxury fabric, such as taffeta and velvet, that are too thick to tie into knots.

What you need

1 square wrap large enough to completely cover the gift and overlap by at least 3" (7.5 cm) after the first fold.

Safety pins, up to 2 yards (2 m) of ribbon, and a brooch (optional).

What to wrap

Almost any gift of any size will work with this wrap. The gift doesn't have to be in a box; if you are wrapping a grouping of gifts, such as toiletries, tie a ribbon around them first so they don't move around inside the wrap.

Fabric notes

With no knots to tie, delicate and decadent fabrics, like taffeta and velvet, may be used to lovely effect. Alternatively, sturdy, thicker fabrics are good choices, as their bulk won't be an issue. Lace can also be fun, but make sure you line it or your wrap will be see-through!

Tips + variations

This wrap is especially useful for flat gifts that come in an envelope: gift cards, cash gifts, and event tickets. A small wrap (page 12) is the right size for most envelopes. Go for a luxury effect, like above, using plush velvet embellished with a rosette or sequined and glittery fabrics, to make any occasion feel like a celebration.

How to do it

1. Lay wrap flat on a diagonal and place box in the center with the top of the box facing down. Turn over corners "a" and "c." Fold "a" and "c" until they meet on top of the box. Fold fabric flush against the side of the box as you would when wrapping a gift in paper.

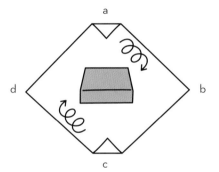

2. Fold corners "b" and "d" over toward the box, tucking in excess fabric so that fabric sits flush against the box. Fold sides up over the box until they meet in the center.

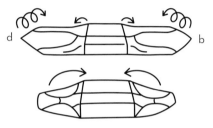

3. Take a large safety pin and secure the layers of fabric by pinning them together at "e." Turn the box over so that the top of the box is facing up.

4. Wrap the ribbon over the width of the top of the box. Turn the box over and twist the ribbon, bringing it lengthwise over the box. Turn the box right side up and tie the ribbon in the center of the box.

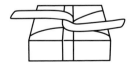

5. Attach an ornament in the center on the gift. Also, make sure the safety pin underneath is hidden.

Bouquet Wrap

Fresh-Cut Flowers

To enhance the beauty of fresh flowers and to avoid packaging waste, bring the Bouquet Wrap with you to the florist like you would a canvas bag to the grocery store. The Bouquet Wrap makes a fantastic hostess gift, and once opened, the wrap can be re-deployed around the vase.

What you need

1 square wrap and ½ to 1 yard (½ to 1 m) of ribbon. A 28"x 28" (71 x 71 cm) wrap is usually large enough for an average bouquet. Use a larger cloth for tall flowers like gladioli.

What to wrap

A bouquet of fresh-cut flowers. Adjust the size of your wrap depending on how large your bouquet is.

Fabric notes

Cotton or linen works best. Choose a pattern that complements the type of flowers, the colors, and the occasion. If the bouquet is a grouping of mixed flowers, opt for a solid color or a small print; if the bouquet is one type of flower, say roses or peonies, use a busier, more colorful pattern.

Place a small piece of plastic wrap around the stems of the flowers so that the fabric does not get wet.

Tips + variations

Wraps are great for decorating unattractive flowerpots. Follow the first two steps for the Bouquet Wrap. For step 3, fold the wrap to the top of the pot, covering it completely. Once the fabric is wrapped around the pot, secure it by tying a ribbon around the middle. Fold the back corner down, over the pot. A 28"x 28" (71 x 71 cm) wrap is a good size for a pot 4" to 7" (10 to 18 cm) high.

For a vase, simply wrap it with the fabric and tie a square knot around the front.

How to do it

1. Lay wrap flat on a diagonal and fold "c" up toward "a" to form a triangle.

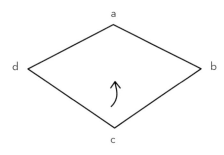

2. Place bouquet of flowers on top of wrap at corner "d." Be sure to wrap a piece of plastic wrap over the ends of the stems first so that the cloth stays dry.

3. Fold wrap up from the bottom by 3" (7.5 cm), over top of the flower stems. Roll the flowers in the wrap starting from "d" and rolling toward "b."

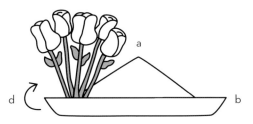

4. Hold wrap together by tying a ribbon around the middle and finishing with a bow.

Soft Wrap

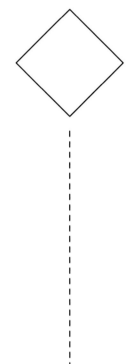

Decoration

Lovely to rest upon but hard to wrap, pillows and cushions are *Wrapagami* favorites. The very easy and attractive Soft Wrap can be done in less than three minutes. Not only does the wrap cover the cushion, but it can also be reused as a cushion cover! Create a wrap with colors that match the pillow inside; then, the recipient can reuse it on another pillow and have a matching set.

What you need

A 36"x 36" (91.5 x 91.5 cm) wrap fits a cushion that is 15"x 15" (38 x 38 cm). The wrap on page 108 is made from many small squares of fabric in different patterns and 1 large square for the attached lining. Cut 49 squares 5½"x5½" (14 x 14 cm)—includes a ¼" (0.6 cm) seam allowance—or find a vintage patchwork piece to use.

What to wrap

A square cushion, adjusting the size of your wrap to the size of the cushion.

Fabric notes

Keeping in mind that the wrap will have a lining, use a cotton that is soft and durable but not too thick. A solid cotton broadcloth works well as the lining and is reasonably priced. Stay away from slippery fabrics, which can be difficult to sew. Choose lightweight fabrics, avoiding anything that has a high pile, such as velvet, in order to achieve clean corners.

Patchwork tips

Use a sewing machine to create your own patchwork piece of fabric for the look you want.

The first thing to keep in mind when sewing a patchwork wrap is to be precise in your cutting and to make sure all squares are the same size. Use a rotary cutter and cutting board with a see-through ruler to help with accuracy (both can be found at quilt shops).

Before picking your fabric, choose a color palette. I chose olive, apple green, coral, and pale pink. Some patterns have all four colors in them, while others have one dominant color. Staying within the color palette allows variety in the patterns—from graphic and modern to old-fashioned florals. The key is to have variety within structure.

Some of the patterns can be all-over prints, like polka dots, while others can be larger scale, more random prints. When cutting the squares of the more random fabrics, crop the pattern differently in each square.

Buy enough fabric of each pattern to use at least one square in each row, horizontally and vertically. For a random arrangement that works, place the patterns in a different order for each row, making sure to include each pattern at least once in all rows. Make sure to plan your layout before you start sewing.

How to do it

1. Lay your finished patchwork fabric flat on a diagonal and place the cushion form in the center.

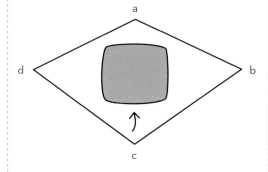

2. Fold "c" up over the cushion so that it covers most of the cushion. Fold the tip of corner "a" over.

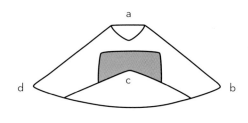

3. Fold "a" over the cushion so that the fold line sits exactly halfway over the cushion.

4. Bring "d" and "b" up and tie together into a square knot over the center of the cushion. Adjust gathers evenly.

Box Cozy Wrap

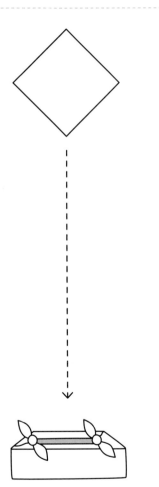

Disguisement

Fabric wraps are a great way to add visual flair to utilitarian objects around the house. Tissue boxes, for example, can be a real eyesore with their unappealing designs, but the Box Cozy Wrap will transform them into a work of art. Choose fabric that matches the mood in the room. When the box is empty, simply untie one half of the wrap, slide the old box out and the new one in, and re-tie. The technique can be applied to most boxes, baskets, or containers, for it is easy to adjust the size of the wrap. Imagine how nice your desk inbox tray and penholder could look!

What you need

1 square wrap. A 20"x 20" (51 x 51 cm) wrap fits a standard tissue box.

What to wrap

Utilitarian boxes, baskets, and containers that are open on the top. Try tissue boxes, small garbage cans, desk accessories, trays, and recycling bins.

Fabric notes

Choose a fabric that will comple-ment the decor of the room.

A medium-weight cotton works best. It is stiff enough to hold the shape of the wrap, yet won't be too bulky when the excess fabric is tucked in. Avoid delicate fabrics that may not hold up to regular use over time.

Tips + variations

A simple penholder, like the one pic-tured, becomes more attractive with this variation on the Box Cozy Wrap.

Another idea is to decorate rectangular baskets that are often used for storage in bedrooms. Use fabric that complements the bedding or curtains. To cover the contents of the basket, simply untuck the fabric on top and pull it across the basket.

How to do it

1. Lay wrap flat as a square and place tissue box in the center with the long side facing you.

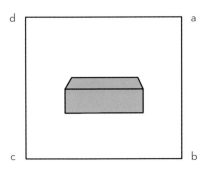

2. Tie "a" and "b" together into a square knot over the top of the box, just before the opening for the tissues.

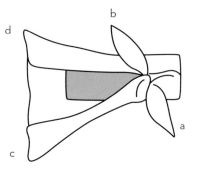

3. Repeat step 2 with "c" and "d."

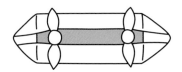

4. Tuck excess fabric under the knots. Fold the sides over to reveal the opening to the tissues. Arrange gathers evenly.

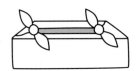

Global Wraps

Journeys

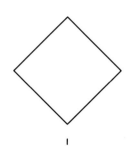

A trip—yours or someone else's—frequently calls for a gift. Fabric brought home from abroad, or chosen for its cultural symbolism, lends a gift an exotic flavor. There are many prints to choose from for handmade wraps, or repurpose a cloth item from afar, such as an Indian sari, a Spanish shawl, an African Kente cloth, or a European tea towel.

What you need

1 square wrap. Size depends on which wrap style you choose and the size of your gift.

What to wrap

Anything goes! Try a souvenir from your travels or an item useful for a traveler-to-be.

Fabric notes

Search for ethnic fabrics when you travel, and keep them for future wraps.

Tips + variations

1. **Khanga Wrap** Vivid, graphic African prints are great for wrapagami. This lively wrap is a snippet from a Tanzanian Khanga cloth printed in traditional African colors and patterns. The Flat Ribbon Wrap on page 100 has a piece of wool yarn embellishing it.

2. **Kilt Wrap** Imagine a box of short-bread wrapped in this traditional Scottish plaid. The Flat Ribbon Wrap from page 100 is held together by a kilt pin.

3. Matryoshka Wrap A kids' fabric with a retro feel, this Russian doll print is perfect for a gift of nesting dolls. This package uses the Bundle Wrap technique on page 86.

5. Flamenco Wrap This dramatic black wrap, embroidered with brightly colored flowers, is ideal for a Spanish-themed wrap, using the Bundle Wrap on page 86.

4. Sari Wrap To capture the vivid colors and decorative feel of an Indian sari, this gift is wrapped in emerald green taffeta and adorned with an ornate ribbon embroidered with gold thread, using the Flat Ribbon Wrap on page 100.

Embellishments

Complement your wrapagami with decorations, trinkets, and ribbon that embellish and entice. Embellishments make your gift feel special and unique.

RIBBON

Ribbon, like fabric, should be reused. High-quality ribbon feels nice, is beautifully designed, and will hold up for many reuses. A ribbon can determine the look of the gift, whether it contrasts with the wrap for a dramatic look, glitters with luxury, or is bright and bold for a playful feel. Avoid disappointment by purchasing extra ribbon, so you have more to play with. It is easier to tie a bow with excess ribbon, cutting off the extra bits at the end, than to fiddle with a piece that is too short.

BUTTERFLIES & BIRDS

Weddings and springtime occasions call for charming little butterflies and birds. They often come with a clip or a wire that makes it easy to attach to the wrap. Typically, you can find little birds and butterflies at craft and stationery stores. For holiday gifts, try seasonal bird ornaments that are meant to clip onto a tree.

TOYS & TRINKETS

Toys that are peeking out or hanging from the gift transform a plain wrap into an adorable one. The Kangaroo Wrap (page 68) shows how little stuffed animals add character to the wrap. Toys and trinkets are extra gifts and will surely be appreciated. They also tie into the theme of the gift and are a prelude to the surprise inside.

SILK FLOWERS

Good quality silk flowers look very real and can bring a touch of elegance to your wrap. Try a branch of pink cherry blossoms or glue a single silk flower to a hair barrette and clip it onto the gift. For a wedding gift, choose the same type of flower as in the bride's bouquet.

JEWELRY & CHARMS

Vintage brooches instantly add sparkle and glamour to a gift. They are also very easy to attach; they simply pin onto the fabric. A long necklace may be draped over the Single Bottle Wrap (page 42) for decoration. Thread a thin ribbon through the hole at the top of a charm, and tie around the gift for someone who collects trinkets.

CHOPSTICKS & LOLLIPOPS

Knots are a great place to slip in long, thin items that can be held in place by tightening a knot. Try a pinwheel, pen, pencil, lollipop, ornate hairpin, or chopsticks. Key chains can be attached by tying a half-square knot, threading a corner through the key chain hole, and completing the square knot.

CARDS & TAGS

Almost all of the wraps in this book have a place where you can attach a gift tag or slip in a greeting card. A tag or card will always enhance the appeal of a wrap.

Reusing Your Wrap

I love the idea that the wrap I use on a friend's birthday present will be passed on to different people. Fabric wraps are gifts in themselves, whether they are reused to wrap another gift or are treasured and saved.

Wrapagami cuts down on waste and embraces the ecologically sound concepts of reusing packaging and recycling fabric. Most fabric is constructed to last a long time; wrapagami allows it to be reused multiple times.

Here are some ways you can reuse the wraps in this book. Before reusing your wrap, you may have to iron the fabric, especially if you are using a different wrap style.

CARRY BAG
Use your wrap as a cloth bag in place of a plastic one for shopping purchases by tying it into the Over-the-Shoulder Wrap (page 62) or Standard Carry Wrap (page 54).

CUSHION COVER
Use the Soft Wrap (page 108) to spontaneously give any room a new look. Start a collection of wraps to pull from to keep your home decor fresh. If you are having a party or would like to have a different look for the holidays, use a wrap on your existing cushions to change their look. The wrap is attractive from both sides, with the knot or plain.

WEARABLE
Wear as a scarf, bandanna, or shawl.

LUNCH BUNDLE
Carry your lunch in a wrap by placing the food in the center and tying the two opposite corners into square knots for a portable lunch bundle. A large wrap is handy for carrying awkward dishes to a potluck.

OUTDOOR ACCESSORY
It's handy to have when hiking to sit on, to carry food in, or to wear as a head scarf to protect yourself from the sun.

ORGANIZING
Bundle loose items in your purse to keep them handy and easy to find. If you forget your sunglasses or mobile phone case, use your wrap to protect fragile items until you get home.

KIDSTUFF
Wraps make great dress-up clothes (think capes and sarongs), blankets for dolls, forts, tea party tablecloths, and tents. At Halloween, make a bag to collect candy in a Halloween print or a fabric that matches the costume.

CRAFTS
Small wraps are perfect for quilting and sewing projects, such as pouches, wallets, purses, toys, and doll clothes.

TABLECLOTH
Large wraps can be used as tablecloths. For a table runner, cut the wrap to the appropriate width and finish the edge.

WALL HANGING
A beautiful piece of fabric can be a work of art, framed or displayed as a wall hanging.

LINING
Lay the wrap inside a basket or box to line it.

HANKY
If you are desperate and can't find a tissue, use it as an old-fashioned hanky.

TRAVEL ACCESSORY
A fabric wrap is a handy item to bring on a trip. Place it on the back of an airplane seat for a clean spot to rest your head, or use your wrap to bundle your socks and underwear to keep them together in your suitcase.

NAPKIN
Most fabric wraps are easy to wash, which makes them great to use as emergency napkins while eating on the go.

Index

Resources

READY TO GO WRAPAGAMI

Furochic™
Furochic™ is available at **www.furochic.com**.
View demonstrations, find inspiration and ideas, and buy wrapagami supplies.

Furoshiki
Traditional Japanese furoshiki can be purchased on the Internet.

www.furoshiki.com
An online resource and shop with reasonably priced furoshiki in mainly Japanese inspired designs.

www.wahooya.com
An online shop featuring Japanese products including furoshiki with traditional Japanese imagery.

www.kakefuda.co.jp
Kakefuda is a furoshiki shop in Kyoto that sells a modern array of beautifully designed furoshiki. Demonstrations are performed for customers who "ooh" and "ahh" when they see the flat square cloths transform into functional and stylish bags and gift wraps. *Note: This website is only in Japanese*

MAKE YOUR OWN WRAPAGAMI

Fabric
Quilt shops are great for finding fun prints from designers like Amy Butler, Heather Bailey, and Kaffe Fassett, and they carry good quality cottons. Your local fabric shops will have a good selection of the basics: velvet, taffeta, silk, and cotton broadcloth. Don't forget to check out the remnant bins for fabric on sale—they usually have pieces large enough to make a square wrapping cloth.

The fabric in *Wrapagami* was purchased at:

Satin Moon Quilt Shop, Victoria, BC
www.satin-moon.com

Purl Patchwork, NYC
www.purlsoho.com

Fabric Tales
www.fabrictales.com

Ribbon, Embellishments & Accessories
For a great selection of ribbons:
www.ribbonjar.com
www.raffit.com

For customized tags:
www.myownlabels.com

Many retailers sell Mokuba ribbons, which are high-quality, beautiful ribbons from Japan.

Search craft stores, stationery stores, and ethnic shops for silk flowers, birds, and butterflies. Bead stores often have charms and trinkets. Novelty and toy stores have a good selection of small gifts to decorate with. Craft, yarn, and fabric stores often carry purse handles. Also, search the Internet for online suppliers.

Credits

PAGE	WRAP	SIZE	FABRIC SUGGESTION
18, 20	Basic Box	28"x28" (71x71 cm)	"Cherry Blossom" Furochic™
23	4-Tie Box	28"x28" (71x71 cm)	"Poppy" Furochic™
24	4-Tie Box	28"x28" (71x71 cm)	"Japanese Garden" Furochic™
26, 28	Double-Knot Box	28"x28" (71x71 cm)	"Kimono" Furochic™
31, 32	Slender Box	28"x28" (71x71 cm)	cotton polka-dot print
34, 36	Single Book	28"x28" (71x71 cm)	"Swirl" Furochic™
39, 40	Double Book	40"x40" (1x1 m)	damask
42, 44	Single Bottle	28"x28" (71x71 cm)	cotton Art Nouveau print
47, 48	Double Bottle	36"x36" (91.5x91.5 cm)	Japanese chirimin crêpe
50	Candlestick	28"x28" (71x71 cm)	cotton paisley print
52	Half-Candlestick	28"x28" (71x71 cm)	cotton paisley print
55	Standard Carry	28"x28" (71x71 cm)	"Elephant Parade" Furochic™
56	Handle	28"x28" (71x71 cm)	"Message" Furochic™
58	Watermelon	38"x38" (1x1 m)	cotton floral print
60	Mini-Watermelon	28"x28" (71x71 cm)	"Wave" Furochic™
63	Over-the-Shoulder	42"x42" (1x1 m)	damask
64	Handbag	42"x42" (1x1 m)	damask
68	Kangaroo	30"x30" (76x76 cm)	pink cotton bunny print
68	Kangaroo	30"x30" (76x76 cm)	blue cotton cloud print
70	Kangaroo	30"x30" (76x76 cm)	monkey print receiving blanket
73, 74	Top-Knot	36"x36" (91.5x91.5 cm)	linen robot wrap
73, 74	Top-Knot	36"x36" (91.5x91.5 cm)	cotton patchwork print
76	Fish-Shape	28"x28" (71x71 cm)	cotton batik
78	Standard Carry	28"x28" (71x71 cm)	cotton underwater print
81, 82	Off-Center	40"x40" (1x1 m)	dupioni silk
84	Round Tin	28"x28" (71x71 cm)	"Holiday Burst" Furochic™
86	Bundle	28"x28" (71x71 cm)	"Holiday Bloom" Furochic™
89	Basket	42"x42" (1x1 m)	cotton bees & clover print
90	Basket	40"x40" (1x1 m)	cotton gingham
92	Roll-and-Tie	25"x25" (63.5x63.5 cm)	cotton geometric pattern
94	Roll-and-Tie	22"x22" (56x56 cm)	cotton bandanna
97	Repurposed	varies	adult medium-size vintage shirt
98	Repurposed	28"x28" (71x71 cm)	vintage silk scarf
100	Flat Ribbon	40"x40" (1x1 m)	taffeta
102	Flat Ribbon	15"x15" (38x38 cm)	velvet
102	Flat Ribbon	15"x15" (38x38 cm)	synthetic sequined fabric
105, 106	Bouquet	28"x28" (71x71 cm)	cotton floral print
108	Soft	36"x36" (91.5x91.5 cm)	cotton homemade patchwork
113, 114	Box Cozy	20"x20" (51x51 cm)	cotton spiral & floral print
116	Basic Box	28"x28" (71x71 cm)	cotton Japanese umbrella print
116	4-Tie Box	28"x28" (71x71 cm)	cotton retro-Chinese print
118	Flat Ribbon	10"x10" (25.5x25.5 cm)	cotton African print
118	Flat Ribbon	15"x15" (38x38 cm)	cotton traditional plaid
119	Bundle	20"x20" (51x51 cm)	cotton Russian doll print
119	Flat Ribbon	20"x20" (51x51 cm)	taffeta
119	Bundle	20"x20" (51x51 cm)	embroidered cotton

About the Author

Born in Toronto, Jennifer Playford grew up in Switzerland, Belgium, and Germany, where she experienced the taste for travel and different cultures that have greatly influenced her art. After university, she lived in London and traveled throughout Africa and Asia before settling in Vancouver. She has worked as a graphic designer and photographer for an African safari company and as a fashion doll-clothing designer for a toy company in Hong Kong.

Jennifer stumbled into illustration* by accident when a friend encouraged her to put together a portfolio after seeing her drawings in a letter. This led to Jennifer's dream job, starting her stationery company, Jenny Wren Paperie, and her reusable fabric gift-wrap line, Furochic™.

Furochic™ started as four silkscreened wraps that were test-launched at the National Stationery Show in New York City in 2007, where it was a finalist for the Best New Products Award. The demand for her wraps was so great that Furochic™ quickly grew into a collection of twelve designs, with international distribution.

Jennifer lives by the beach in Victoria on Vancouver Island with her husband, Scott, and two children, Ava and Oliver.

*As an illustrator, Jennifer is represented by Magnet Reps and has worked with some great clients, including La Perla, Delta Airlines, Klutz Publishing, Running Press, Random House, *Waitrose Food Illustrated*, Coca Cola, *Los Angeles Times*, Aussie Haircare, Virgin, Natural Health, and *CosmoGirl*. She has also received honors from *Communication Arts* and *American Illustration*, and her work has appeared in the books *Pattern Design, Applications & Variations* and *The Big Book of Illustration Ideas*.